THIS BOOK IS PRESENTED TO:

_____

IT WAS GIVEN TO YOU BY:

_____

ON THIS SPECIAL DAY:

_____

GOD IS IN THE SMALL STUFF

AN IMPRINT OF
BARBOUR PUBLISHING

GOD IS IN THE
SMALL STUFF
FOR KIDS

BRUCE & STAN
Illustrated by Phil Smouse

Published by Promise Kids, an imprint of Barbour Publishing, Inc., P.O. Box 719, Uhrichsville, Ohio 44683 www.promisepress.com

Member of the
Evangelical Christian
Publishers Association

Printed in China.

CONTENTS

INTRODUCTION

God is important. He made the whole world. He made everything in the world. God knows everything that happened a long time ago. He knows everything that is happening right now. God even knows what is going to happen tomorrow. God knows everything about everything.

God is very important, but He always has time for you. God loves you. You are very special to God.

God cares about you and your life. He cares about the big things, like the things that make you cry. God cares when you are afraid. He likes it when you are happy.

God also cares about the small stuff in your life. He is interested in the way you treat your brother or sister. He cares about how you feel when you go to bed at night. God cares about you when you sleep. God cares about you when you wake up in the morning. He likes to hear you laugh when you are playing games or just being silly.

Some people think that God only pays attention to them when they go to church. They think that He is too busy to care about them when they are at home. Those people are making a big mistake. Sure, God knows when we are in church. But He is also watching over us all of the other times, too.

God is big. . .big enough to be with you wherever you go. Because He loves you so much, He is interested in everything that happens in your life. God cares about the big stuff and the small stuff.

Bruce & Stan

Surely you know. Surely you have heard. The Lord is the God who lives forever, who created all the world. He does not become tired or need to rest. No one can understand how great his wisdom is.

Isaiah 40:28

WHAT IS GOD LIKE?

What is God like? Do you ever wonder about that? Lots of people do. It is okay to wonder about God. He likes it when we think about Him.

We cannot know everything about God. But we can learn a lot about Him because there are many clues. The stories in the Bible tell a lot about God. But there are more clues than just the Bible.

- Look up in the sky at nighttime and see the stars. God made them all. The sky can give you a clue about how big God is.

- Think about the ocean and the waves. They are clues about how strong God is.

- Play with a puppy or a kitten. God knew that we would have fun with pets. That is a clue about how caring God is.

But wait—there is another clue. This is the best one of all. Ask a grown-up for a big hug. You know, the kind where they wrap their arms around you and hold you tight until your eyes pop out. Think about how good you feel when you are being hugged. God knew that you would like being hugged. That is a clue about how loving God is.

The next time you are wondering about God, remember the clues.

...IN THE SMALL STUFF

- God knows all about you.
  Learn about God.

- Clues about God are easy to find
  if you look for them.

- You can learn a lot about God
  if you think about Him.

LET'S TALK ABOUT THE SMALL STUFF

- What do you think God is like?

- Can you think of a clue about God?

- What makes God laugh?

We pray. . .that
you will live
the kind of life that
honors and pleases
the Lord in
every way.

Colossians 1:9–10

BE FRIENDS WITH GOD

God wants to be your friend. Isn't that great? He will be the best friend you'll ever have. He will always help you. He will never be mean to you. He won't move away from you. He will be your friend for your whole life.

Do you want to know what makes God such a good friend? He isn't bossy or pushy. He isn't a bully. He lets you decide about your friendship with Him. God wants to be best friends with you. But He is not going to make you be friends with Him. It is up to you.

Do you want to know how you can be better friends with God? It's easy. Spend time with Him. That is how you make friends with other kids. You talk and play with them. It is the same way with God.

You cannot play soccer with God. But you can think about God each day. (You are doing that right now!) You can talk with God during the day. Thank Him for the things He has given to you. Tell Him what you are worried about. Talk to Him just like He is your friend. . .because He is.

...iN THE SMALL STUFF

- God is very polite. He lets you decide if you want to be friends with Him.

- Being friends with God takes time, but it is worth it.

- Get to know God, so He can be your best friend.

- Life is more fun with God as your friend.

LET'S TALK ABOUT THE
SMALL STUFF

- Why do you like being friends with God?

- How can you become better friends with God?

- What do you think are things that God likes best about you?

This is what real love is:
It is not our love for God;
it is God's love for us.

1 John 4:10

GOD LOVES YOU

Love is a funny word. It can mean different things. You might say, "I love playing in the rain." You could say, "I love eating pizza." But do you really love those things? You like the rain. You probably enjoy having a tummy full of pizza. But you do not love those things like you love things that are alive.

Love is serious. Love means you want the best for others. Love means you are willing to give up something to help them.

- You love your pet. You work hard to take care of it. You feed your pet. You make sure your pet stays clean and has a nice place to sleep.

- You love your parents. That is why you will do what they ask even if you would rather do something else.

- Your parents love you. That is why they work hard at a job and around the house. They want you to have a nice life.

When you love someone, you aren't selfish. You do things for them instead of always wanting your own way.

God is the best example of true love. He is never selfish. He is always doing what is best for you. The Bible says that God loves you, and that's the truth. He really does.

...iN THE SMALL STUFF

- God loves you. . . even when you don't act like you love Him.

- Because God loves you so much, you should love Him back.

- You are a special person because God loves you. Don't ever forget that.

- God's love never runs out.

LET'S TALK ABOUT THE
SMALL
STUFF

- Name something God has done for you because He loves you so much.

- What are some ways that you can show God that you love Him?

- Think of three things that you *like* and three things that you *love.*

*"I am the Lord your God,
who teaches you to
do what is good,
who leads you in
the way you should go."*

Isaiah 48:17

FOLLOW THE LEADER

Have you ever played "Follow the Leader"? That is the game where you copy what someone else is doing. If the leader turns to the right, then you turn to the right. If the leader turns to the left, then you turn to the left. You have to watch the leader if you want to be good at the game. You will get mixed up and go the wrong way if you are not paying attention.

Life is like that. It is filled with choices. You have to decide what is the right thing to do. You have to decide what is the wrong thing to do.

Making choices is easier if God is your leader. There are many ways He will show you what to do. Sometimes you can find an answer in the Bible. Sometimes your parent or another grown-up will give you advice. Sometimes God gives you a feeling in your heart to let you know what you should do.

Think about God when you have a choice to make. Think about God when you have a problem. Let Him be your leader. Think about what God would want you to do. Then do it. Play "Follow the Leader" with God.

...IN THE SMALL STUFF

- God wants to be your leader every day.

- Follow God when you have a problem.

- It is easier to follow God when you think about Him every day.

- Think about God before you do something.

LET'S TALK ABOUT THE
SMALL STUFF

- Tell about a time when you followed God and did what He wanted you to do.

- What grown-up helps you know what God wants you to do?

- Has God ever given you a feeling in your heart about doing the right thing?

*We must always
thank God for you. . .
because your faith
is growing more
and more.*

2 Thessalonians 1:3

GOD IS
WATCHING YOU GROW

What did you look like when you were a baby? Look at some of your baby pictures. Where you big and chubby? Were you little and wrinkled? One thing is for sure: You were small.

You did not stay small. You grew. You *really* grew. When you were a baby, everybody carried you around like a loaf of bread. Now you are so big—and you weigh more than a sack of cement.

God has been watching you grow. He enjoyed seeing you grow from a tiny baby into a big kid. But God wants you to grow in a different way, too.

When your body grows bigger, that is called *physical* growth. That kind of growth is important. God also wants you to grow *spiritually.* That kind of growth happens when you learn more about God.

You grow spiritually when you let God be an important part of your life. You get spiritually "bigger" when you obey God and show His love to others.

Physical growth is important. If you stayed the size of a baby, you could not ride a bike or play sports. Spiritual growth is important, too. When it comes to knowing and loving God, you do not want to stay a baby. Don't forget to grow with God.

...IN THE SMALL STUFF

- God likes to see you grow physically.
  God likes to see you grow spiritually.

- You will never grow too big for God.

- You will grow bigger and taller all by
  yourself. It just happens.

- If you want to grow in God,
  you are going to
  have to work at it.

LET'S TALK ABOUT THE
SMALL STUFF

- Draw a picture of what you looked like as a baby. Then draw a picture of what you will look like as a grown-up.

- Maybe you have a chart on the wall to show how you have grown taller. What are some things you do that show you have grown spiritually?

- Exercise, sleep, and eating good food help you grow physically. What do you need to help you grow spiritually?

*Your word is like
a lamp for my feet
and a light
for my path.*

Psalm 119:105

GOD HAS A MESSAGE FOR YOU

You have books in your room. Your parents have books in the house. Think about all of the rooms and houses with books. Think about all of the libraries with books. You could never count all of the books in the world.

There is one book that is more popular than any other book. It is the world's favorite book of all time. It is the Bible.

The Bible is full of true-life adventure stories. But that is not the only reason it is so popular. The author of the Bible is God. God told certain people what to write, and they wrote it down exactly as God said it.

Do you like to get mail? What if God was sending you a letter? You would check the mailbox every hour until God's letter came. What if God was sending you an E-mail? You would check the computer until God's E-mail came.

God has not sent you a letter. God has not sent you an E-mail. God has sent you something even better. God has sent you a personal message. It is in the Bible. Everything that He wants you to know is written there.

Find out God's personal message to you. Read the Bible every day.

...iN THE SMALL STUFF

- Read the Bible if you want to know what God is saying to you.

- You won't know God's personal message to you if you leave the Bible on the shelf.

- The Bible is better than television—because it doesn't have commercials.

- If you can't read the Bible for yourself, ask a grown-up to read it to you. That way you can hear God's message, and the grown-up can, too.

LET'S TALK ABOUT THE
SMALL STUFF

- What is your favorite Bible story? What does that story teach you about God?

- You can read the Bible at any time and in any place. But most people have their favorite place and time. What would be a good time and place for you to read the Bible for a few minutes each day?

- Where would be a good place to keep your Bible so you remember it read it?

God says,
"Be quiet and know
that I am God."

Psalm 46:10

GOD GOES WITH YOU

Everybody is very busy. Your parents are busy at work and at home. Do you have older brothers or sisters? They are busy at school. You are busy with your own stuff.

Everybody is rushing from one place to another. Even grandparents are busy. But they don't seem as busy because they move a little slower.

Wherever you go, wherever you are, God is with you. You never leave Him behind because He goes with you.

You might think about God the most when you are at home or at church. But God is also with you when you are riding in the car. God is with you at the store or on the playground.

God is never too busy to listen to you. You don't have to ask to talk with Him. Just stop being busy for a moment and say a prayer to Him. It is as easy as that. You might be busy, but God isn't. He is never too busy for you.

Do you ever get nervous when everyone is so busy? That is the best time to say a prayer. God will give you a feeling that everything is okay because He is with you. You will feel better when you remember that God is with you. Then all of the rushing around won't seem so bad.

...IN THE SMALL STUFF

- Even though you are busy, God is never too busy for you.

- Wherever you go, God goes with you.

- It's easy to talk with God. You can do it anytime. But it is usually best if you slow down for a moment, so you have a chance to listen to Him.

LET'S TALK ABOUT THE
SMALL STUFF

- When were you nervous but God made you feel better?

- Can you think of some places you have gone where God has been with you?

- When do you get the busiest and need to think about God?

*The Lord sees
the good people
and listens to
their prayers.*

1 Peter 3:12

TALKING WITH GOD

What if no one ever talked? Think about how crazy that would be. No one would talk in your house. No one would talk on the phone. No one would talk in the stores. And it would be boring to watch TV because people would just move around without making noise. It would be a very quiet world. There would be nothing to hear. You wouldn't even need your ears.

But it would be lonely. You couldn't tell your stories. You couldn't tell your jokes. You couldn't ask your parents for help. You couldn't even say, "Save some cookies for me," when your dad was eating the whole bag of them.

Talking is fun. When you talk, you can tell people things. You can tell them what you want. You can let them know how you feel.

Do you ever want to talk, but no one wants to listen to you? Sometimes people are busy doing something else and can't listen when you want to talk. But not God. He always has time for you. And He loves to hear you talk.

Talking to God is called "praying." You can pray to God about anything. He wants to know what you are thinking about. You can tell Him what you are thankful for. You can tell Him what you are worried about. You can even tell Him a joke because He likes to laugh.

Don't forget to talk to God. He is listening.

...IN THE SMALL STUFF

- Praying to God is like talking to a friend.

- God loves the sound of your voice.

- Start each day by saying "good morning" to God.

    - End each day by saying "good night" to God.

LET'S TALK ABOUT THE
SMALL STUFF

- You can ask God to help other people. Who do you know who needs special help from God?

- You can ask God to help you. What do you want to pray for?

- When you are talking to God, you can thank Him for the things He has given to you. Pray right now and thank God for three of them.

*You should not
stay away from
the church meetings. . .
you should meet
together and
encourage each other.*

Hebrews 10:25

YOU'RE PART OF GOD'S GIANT FAMILY

How many people are in your family? Can you count them? Your family is bigger than the people who live in your house. Don't forget about your grandparents. What about your uncles and aunts? And what about your cousins? Wow! There are lots of people in your family.

God has a big family, too. His family is bigger than yours. He has a giant family. That doesn't mean His family is full of giants. It means that there are many, many, many people in God's family.

Everyone who loves God is part of His family. Because you love God, you are part of His family, too.

Are there times when all of the people in your family get together? Does that happen at birthdays and holidays? The people in God's family like to meet together, too. But nobody's house is big enough to hold God's giant family. That is why there are church buildings. The people in God's family meet at the churches. They go to church so they can all be together. At church they sing songs to God and learn more about Him.

You are an important part of God's family. You can see the rest of God's giant family at church.

...IN THE SMALL STUFF

- God is so glad that you are part of His giant family.

- You can see some of the other people in God's giant family at your church.

- There are people in God's giant family who live all around the world.

- You are part of God's family because you love Him. Who else do you know who is in God's family?

- Draw a picture of your church.

- What is your favorite thing about going to church?

The heavens tell
the glory of God,
and the skies
announce what
his hands have made.

Psalm 19:1

Look what God made

Do you like to draw pictures? Do you like to color? Maybe you have some of your pictures on the wall in your bedroom. Maybe some of your artwork is on the refrigerator in your kitchen.

Have you ever made something out of clay? Or what about Legos? Making things is fun.

You aren't the only one who likes to make things. God does, too. God made the whole world: the sky, the sun, the moon, the stars, the land, and the ocean. God also made all of the animals: the birds, the elephants, the fish, the bears, and all of the rest of them. God even made those funny little wiener dogs.

God loves you so much that He made a nice world for you to enjoy. He made the world big to give you lots of room to run. He made the world beautiful to give you lots to see. He made pets for you to play with. And He made many things in the world for you to eat so you won't go hungry.

The next time you go outside, look at all the things God made. He made all of those things for you.

...iN THE SMaLL STUFF

- When you look in the sky, you can see what God made.

- When you look at the land, you can see what God made.

- When you look in a mirror, you can see what God made.

- All that God made,
  He made for you.

- Draw a picture of something that God made.

- Go into the yard and find something pretty that God made. Put it on the refrigerator next to something that you made.

- What are some of your favorite things that God made for you?

_____

_____

_____

Lord, teach me
your ways, and guide me
to do what is right.

Psalm 27:11

CHOOSE TO DO
THE RIGHT THING

There are lots of things you get to choose. You can choose what shirt to wear. You can choose what cereal you are going to eat. You can choose what game you want to play. And when your mom or dad buys you an ice cream cone, you get to choose between lots of different flavors.

There are other choices you get to make. Almost every day you make choices between doing the right thing or doing the wrong thing. The right thing is obeying what your parents tell you to do. When you disobey your parents or break the rules, then you are doing the wrong thing.

Your parents want you to do the right thing all the time. God wants you to do the right thing, too.

Parents make rules so that you will be safe. They know the best way for you to have fun. When you follow the rules, you will be happy. But if you break the rules, you will feel bad because you did the wrong thing.

Always choose to do the right thing. It will make your parents happy. It will make God happy. And it will make you happy, too.

...iN THE SMALL STUFF

- Choosing to do the right thing is the best thing to do.

- Always ask yourself: "What would my parents want me to do?"

- Always ask yourself: "What would God want me to do?"

LET'S TALK ABOUT THE
SMALL STUFF

- Was there ever a time when you chose to do the wrong thing? How did that make you feel?

- Was there ever a time when you chose to do the right thing? How did that make you feel?

- What are some of the rules that your parent made so that you can be safe and have fun?

*In your lives
you must think
and act like
Christ Jesus.*

Philippians 2:5

BE LiKE jESUS

Who do you want to be like? Do you want to be just like your mom or dad? Do you put their big shoes on your feet and walk around the house? Do you copy what they say? Do you pretend to be just like them? It is a good idea to be like your parents.

Here is another good idea. Try to be like Jesus. He said we should copy Him and do the things that He did.

The Bible tells the stories about Jesus. If you know the stories about Him, then you can copy what He did. Those stories tell us that He was kind and loving. He always did the right thing. He helped other people.

You can be like Jesus and copy the things that He did. You can be nice to other kids. Maybe you will be playing with some friends, but another kid doesn't have anyone to play with. You can ask that kid to play with you and your friends. That is what Jesus would have done.

You can also be like Jesus if you are helpful at home. Maybe there is a chore that you can do so your parents won't have to. Maybe you can pick your toys up off the floor or help with the dishes.

Every time that you do something nice, you are showing love to another person. Showing love is exactly what Jesus did. When you show love, you are being just like Jesus.

...iN THE SMALL STUFF

- Learn about Jesus so you can copy Him.

- When you do nice things for other people, you are being just like Jesus.

- Being like Jesus will make you feel good inside.

- What are some nice things you can do for someone else?

- How can you help around the house?

- What is one of your favorite stories about Jesus? What did Jesus do in that story? How can you copy what Jesus did in that story?

*Wise children
take their parents' advice.*

Proverbs 13:1

LISTEN TO YOUR PARENTS

The wisest man who ever lived was King Solomon. He lived many years ago. He prayed to God and asked for wisdom. Wisdom is knowing the best thing to do. God made King Solomon very wise.

King Solomon wrote a book. It is the Book of Proverbs in the Bible. The king put much of his wisdom in the book. When we read the Book of Proverbs, we can learn from the smartest man who ever lived.

The verse at the beginning of this chapter was written by King Solomon. He said that children are wise if they follow the advice of their parents.

Think about that. The smartest man who ever lived said that you can be smart, too. All you have to do is follow the advice of your parents. Listen to what they have to say. They are older, so they know a lot of things that you haven't learned yet.

As you grow older, you will know more. When you get to be a grown-up, you may know as much as your parents. Maybe you will even be smarter than they are. But you are not there yet. So, for right now, you should listen to what your parents say. It's a smart thing to do. The smartest man who ever lived said so.

...iN THE SMaLL STUFF

- Your parents know a lot more than you might think they know.

- As you grow older you learn more. Your parents are older, so they know a lot.

- If you don't know something, ask your mom or dad.

- Who is the smartest person that you know?

- Ask your mom or dad what they learned from their parents (your grandparents).

- Ask your mom or dad a question about God.

There is one thing
I always do. . . . I keep
trying to reach the goal
and get the prize for which
God called me.

Philippians 3:13–14

ONE DAY AT A TIME

If you were in a race with a baby, you would win. You can run much faster than a baby. Babies can't even run. They can't even walk. They can only crawl.

A long time ago, you were a baby. You could not run when you were a baby. You could only crawl. But each day you got a little stronger. When you got strong enough, you started to walk. Then you started to run. Now you can run so fast your parents have a hard time catching you.

If you practice running, you can get a little faster every day. But you have to work at it.

The same thing is true about being good. You can be a better person every day if you try hard. When you were a baby, you did not know the right things to do. But you started to learn. Now you are much older. So now you know a lot about being good and following the rules. But you can get even better—if you work at it.

Each day you can know more about God. Knowing more about Him will help you be a better person. Each day you can try your hardest to do the right thing. Little by little, day by day, you will be learning and doing the things that please God.

This means doing the right thing in the small stuff as well as in the big stuff.

...IN THE SMALL STUFF

- Being a better person is like running. It won't happen unless you try it.

- Every day, ask God to help you be a better kid.

- Never give up. Always keep trying.

LET'S TALK ABOUT THE
SMALL STUFF

- Finish this sentence: "I can run faster than a _____."

- Can you run a little faster every day? Can you be a better person every day?

- How can God help you be a better person tomorrow?

*Training your body helps you
in some ways. . . .*

_____

1 Timothy 4:8

TAKE CARE OF YOUR BODY

God cares most about the kind of person you are on the *inside*. He wants you to *think* about Him with your *brain*. He wants you to *love* Him with your *heart*.

But God also cares about you on the outside: He cares about your body. It has to last you a long time, so He wants you to take care of it.

God wants you to take care of your body.

- You should keep it clean. That means using soap and water every day.

- You should give it lots of exercise. That means that you might have to stop watching TV and start playing some games outside.

- You should feed it good food. That means you might have to put down the cupcake and grab a banana.

Do you have a dog or a cat as a pet? You don't let your pet stay dirty and stinky all of the time. You don't keep it in a box all day without the chance to stretch its legs. And you don't give it dirt to eat. Of course not. Pets need to be treated with love and the proper care.

Your body is more important than any pet. Make sure that you are being nice to your own body. Take care of your body. It is one of God's special gifts to you.

...iN THE SMALL STUFF

- You'll feel better if you eat better.

- When you feel better, you can play harder.

- When you can play harder, you can have more fun.

- What are some good-for-you foods that you like to eat?

- What are some ways that you can take better care of your body?

- Draw a picture of you now. Draw a picture of how you will look if you eat better, get more sleep, and play outside every day.

*Do all you can
to live a peaceful life.*

1 Thessalonians 4:11

GET ALONG WITH OTHERS

Most games are more fun to play with other kids. Kids like to play together in groups. Do you? Sometimes, you need a big group of kids to play a game. Other times, you can play with just one or two friends.

Playing with other kids can be lots of fun. But sometimes it isn't fun if someone is selfish or mean. If one person hogs the ball or won't share the toy, then the other kids can't have any fun.

Whenever you are playing with others, don't be a selfish kid. Don't be the mean kid. You should be the one who helps everybody have fun. If they are having more fun, you will have more fun.

There are lots of ways that you can help other people have fun when you are with them:

- When you are playing a game, make sure everyone gets a turn.

- Take turns choosing what games you will play.

- When you are watching TV, make sure everyone gets a good seat. Don't hog the best pillows.

God is pleased when you try to get along with other kids. He wants you to try your best to make other people happy.

...IN THE SMALL STUFF

- Other kids will want to play with you if you are nice to them.

- It is more fun to play nicely with other kids than to fight with them.

- Being kind to others is the most fun of all.

LET'S TALK ABOUT THE
SMALL STUFF

- Who are the friends that you most like to play with?

- Has anyone ever been mean to you when you were playing? How did that make you feel?

- Has anyone ever been nice to you when you were playing? How did that make you feel?

*The thing you
should want most
is. . .doing what
God wants.*

Matthew 6:33

DOING THE SPECIAL STUFF

You are a special person. God loves you, and that makes you special. Your parents and the other people in your family love you. That makes you special, too.

You are a special person, so you should be doing special things. God wants you to do special things. He will help you do them.

You are doing special things when you are kind to other people. You can be kind in many different ways.

Helping is a great way of doing something special. Do you have a friend who needs your help? Is there something around the house that you can do for your parents? What about helping your brother or sister?

Being nice is another great way of doing something special. Asking a friend to play with you is a nice and special thing to do. Drawing a picture or making a gift for a grandparent is a nice thing to do. Doing nice things for other people is very special.

There are lots of special things that you can do each day. You can do special things with your friends—like playing with them. You can do special things with your parents—like singing with your mom or tickling your dad when he falls asleep in front of the TV. And you can even do some special things with God—like praying to Him.

You are a special person. God wants you to have fun doing special things.

...IN THE SMALL STUFF

- Having fun with others is a special thing to do.

- Being nice to others is a special thing to do.

- Helping others is a special thing to do.

- Do something special every day.

LET'S TALK ABOUT THE
SMALL STUFF

- Tell about the time when someone did something special for you.

- Who are the people you can do special things for?

- What are some of the special things that you can do for them?

*Be generous and
ready to share.*

1 Timothy 6:18

SHARE WHAT YOU HAVE

Y ou have lots of stuff. Lots of clothes and lots of toys. God has been very kind to you. He has helped your parents give you lots of stuff.

There are many kids who don't have as much as you. Some kids don't have warm coats to wear in the winter. Some kids don't have enough food to eat—they are always hungry. Some kids don't have any toys to play with.

Some of these kids who need help live far away. Some live in your town.

You can help these other kids by sharing your toys and clothes with them. Don't throw your old toys and clothes away. Share them with other kids who do not have as much as you. Maybe your church has a way to get your stuff to these kids. Your mom and dad might know ways to do it, too.

Always be thinking about what you can share with others.

Don't just share the broken toys. You wouldn't like to get a broken toy from someone. Share something that will be fun for another kid to play with.

God has given many things to you. He wants you to give some of your things to others. You will make other kids very happy when you share your toys and clothes with them. Sharing will make you happy, too.

...IN THE SMALL STUFF

- Sometimes sharing is more fun than getting.

- God gives to you so you can give to others.

- There is always someone who has less than you.

- Be thankful for what you have by sharing what you have.

SMALL STUFF

- Take a good look around your room. What are some of your toys that you can give to other kids who don't have any?

- Take a good look in your closet and in your drawers. What clothes can you give to other kids who don't have enough to wear?

- Pretend you are a kid who doesn't have any toys. What will it be like when that kid gets one of the toys that you are sharing? What will that kid think?

"So I tell you, don't worry
about the food or drink you
need to live, or about the clothes
you need for your body. Life
is more than food, and the
body is more than clothes."

Matthew 6:25

DON'T WORRY

Do you know what it means to worry? It means you aren't sure about something. Maybe you worry about your dad when he goes places. Will he be safe? You feel better when you are with him.

Maybe you worry about things at night. When it's dark, you hear noises. What is that sound? Should you ask for help? You want to be brave.

Maybe you worry about your friends. Will they laugh at your new joke? Will they like your new shoes? Or will they make fun of you?

It's okay to worry about your dad. It's okay to worry about the dark. It's okay to worry about your friends. We all worry. But you should not worry too much. Too much worry can hurt you.

How can worry hurt you? Worry can make you feel sick—it will make your stomach do flip-flops. And worry can turn you away from God. You cannot worry and trust

God at the same time. When you worry, you are telling God: "I don't trust You." When you trust God, you are telling Him: "I believe in You and I know You will take care of me."

Jesus talked about worry. He said that worry doesn't make your life better. Jesus said that we should trust God.

God takes care of the birds. God takes care of the flowers. Most of all, God takes care of you! So the next time you worry, tell God you trust Him to take care of you.

...IN THE SMALL STUFF

- Your worries will go away if you trust God.

- The less you worry, the better you will feel.

- Worry doesn't change things.

- Prayer changes things.

- When you start to worry, start to pray.

LET'S TALK ABOUT THE
SMALL STUFF

- When was the last time you were really worried?

- How does God help you when you worry?

- What does it mean to trust God?

*When you have
many kinds of troubles,
you should be full of joy.*

_____

James 1:2

TROUBLE IS GOOD

There are different kinds of trouble. Sometimes you get into trouble. You do something you should not do, or you make trouble for other people. This is not the good kind of trouble.

There is another kind of trouble. This is when things happen to you. Someone takes your bike. You get sick, or someone you love gets sick. Your family has to move when you don't want to. This kind of trouble can make you strong.

Here is why. God knows about trouble. He is ready to help you when trouble comes. If you pray and ask God to help you, He will answer.

God knows about trouble because of Jesus. Jesus is God's only Son. Jesus came to earth to die for our sins. Jesus knew trouble. But Jesus defeated His trouble when He came back to life. Jesus defeated trouble for you, too.

So when trouble comes your way, remember Jesus. God will help you because of Jesus. God may not take away your trouble. But He promises to help you through your trouble. That's what God did for Jesus. That's what God will do for you.

After your trouble is over, you will be stronger. You will have more patience. You will be smarter. And you will trust God to help you next time trouble comes.

...IN THE SMALL STUFF

- Learn from your troubles.

- If God doesn't take your trouble away, He will help you get through it.

- It feels good when troubles are over.

LET'S TALK ABOUT THE
SMALL STUFF

- What happens when you get into trouble?

- How do you feel when the trouble isn't your fault?

- Do you know somebody who used to have trouble, but is all right now?

*God is the Father
who is full of mercy
and all comfort.*

_____

2 Corinthians 1:3

GOD WILL COMFORT YOU

Comfort is a pretty neat thing. Comfort is what you need when you get hurt—when you fall off your bike, or when somebody makes fun of you.

Who gives you comfort? Does your mother help you when you fall? Does your father help you when you worry? Of course they do. Your parents love you.

Your parents love you a lot. But God loves you even more. You can't see God. But God sees you. He knows when you hurt. He knows when you worry. He wants to comfort you.

Some people blame God when they hurt. Don't do that. God doesn't cause pain. God doesn't cause trouble. Sometimes He lets you have pain and trouble so you will grow strong. But God doesn't cause bad things. God wants to give you comfort.

How does God do this? He gives you peace inside. God helps you feel better. He stays close beside you. That's how God comforts you. We know this because God said so in the Bible.

Are you ever lonely? God is your friend. Do you ever worry? God can help you.

God comforts you, and you can comfort others. Tell them about God. Tell them how He has helped you. Tell them that God isn't like Santa Claus. God is real. God offers real help.

...IN THE SMALL STUFF

- God is close to you even if you don't feel close to Him.

- One way God comforts you is through the Bible.

- A friend is someone who comforts you.

- You don't need words
  to comfort a friend.

LET'S TALK ABOUT THE
SMALL STUFF

- Talk about the last time you really got hurt.

- Who gave you the most comfort?

- How can God comfort you when you can't see Him?

*Happy is the one
who reads the words
of God's message.*

Revelation 1:3

LEARN TO READ

Let's talk about books. We know you like to read books. You are reading this book (and the people who wrote it are glad!).

People who read books grow on the inside. People who don't read books don't grow on the inside. It's that simple. Because you are reading, you are growing.

Think where you would be without books. You would be like a ship in the ocean without a map. You could go places, but you would not know where to go. Books help to guide you.

- Books tell you about people.
  They help you become a better person.

- Books tell you about places.
  They help you enjoy the world.

- Books tell you about things. They help you learn more than you know.

All books are important. But the most important book is the Bible. God wrote the Bible. When you read the Bible, you learn about God. It's that simple.

The words of the Bible are the words of God. They are valuable. King David wrote: "They are worth more than gold" (Psalm 19:10). Another time he wrote: "Your word is like a lamp for my feet and a light for my way" (Psalm 119:105). David loved the Bible.

Here's another good thing about reading the Bible. It makes you happy! So keep reading. And learn to read better. You will learn more, and you will feel better.

...IN THE SMALL STUFF

- The person who does not read is no better than the person who cannot read.

- Read before you go to bed at night.

- Try reading books more than you watch TV.

LET'S TALK ABOUT THE
SMALL STUFF

- What is the best book you ever read?

- Why is reading books better than watching TV?

- How do you think God wrote the Bible?

*You yourselves
are our letter,
written on our hearts,
known and read
by everyone.*

2 Corinthians 3:2

LEARN TO WRITE

Many people like to read. Not many people like to write. Writing is harder than reading. Others might read what you write. That bothers some people.

You have to write in school. First you learn to print letters in the alphabet. Then you connect the letters to make words. Then you combine words to make sentences. That is how you write.

Actually, writing is more than putting words together. Writing is how you tell stories. Writing is how you share your feelings.

Do you want to be a writer? Don't worry about writing a book. Start small—by keeping a journal. A journal starts out as a blank book. There's no writing in it. You are the only one who can write in your journal.

You can also write in your computer. Start a file and call it "Journal." Or you can E-mail your friends. That is writing. You may want to start a personal Web page. This way other people can read what you write.

Write about your day. Write about the people you meet. Write about your family. Write about how you feel about God. Write about what He is doing in the small stuff of your life. God likes it when you write about Him.

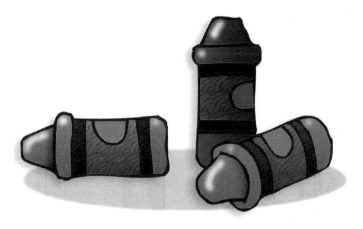

...IN THE SMALL STUFF

- Practice writing by writing letters to your friends.

- Learn a new word every day, and then write it down.

- Write thank-you notes to people when they give you stuff.

- Good writers are good readers.

LET'S TALK ABOUT THE
SMALL STUFF

- What kind of person are you? Write about yourself in the space below.

- Why does God like it when you write about Him?

- Imagine having your own Web page. What would it look like?

*Always be willing to listen
and slow to speak.*

James 1:19

LISTEN
MORE THAN YOU TALK

Do you like to talk? Talking is important. Do you like to listen? Listening is even more important. When you were a baby, you listened before you could talk. That's how you learned how to do stuff.

It's the same now. You still need to listen before you talk. That's how you learn how to do even more stuff. You also learn about other people by listening to them.

Ask them questions such as: What is your favorite color? What games do you like to play? Do you have a favorite song? Do you go to church?

You will make new friends when you listen more than you talk. Your friends will think you are very wise. They will start to ask you questions. People who talk a lot don't seem very wise. They just think they are.

Listening will help you more than talking will. Listen to your parents, your teachers, your friends. You can listen to God, too. You won't hear God's voice out loud, but you will feel God in your heart, after you have read His words in the Bible. He will give you peace if you listen to Him.

...IN THE SMALL STUFF

- Ask questions first. Talk later.

- Think about your questions before you ask them.

- Look at people when they talk to you. It shows you are really listening.

- It's easier to listen to God when it's quiet.

LET'S TALK ABOUT THE
SMALL STUFF

- Write down three questions you could ask your best friend.

- Do you have a quiet place where you can listen to God?

- Who is the best listener you know?

So encourage each other
and build each other up,
just as you are already doing.

1 Thessalonians 5:11 NLT

THE GIFT OF ENCOURAGEMENT

It's fun to get a gift. It's more fun to give a gift. You enjoy making others happy, don't you?

Most gifts cost money. Some gifts cost a lot of money. Video games cost a lot—but they are only fun for a while. We have a gift idea for you. This gift does not cost anything—it's free. It is the gift of encouragement.

- You don't have to shop for encouragement.
- You don't have to gift wrap encouragement.
- Encouragement does not need batteries.
- Encouragement lasts a long, long time.

Here is how you encourage someone. You tell a friend you are happy when he is happy. You tell a friend you are sad when she is sad. Or you tell a friend he can do well when he does not think he can.

Encouragement is the opposite of discouragement. Kind words are encouraging words. Mean words are discouraging.

You can encourage someone by talking. You can encourage someone by writing a note. You can encourage someone by sending an E-mail. No one ever gets too much encouragement.

...iN THE SMALL STUFF

- When you make others feel good, you will feel good.

- Compliment people, but don't overdo it.

- Encouragement helps other people do better.

- Be kind to unkind people. It gets to them.

- What is the nicest thing anybody has ever said to you? How did it make you feel?

- What is the meanest thing anybody ever said to you? How did it make you feel?

- Think of a time when your mom encouraged you. What did she say?

*Anyone who has
the gift of being
a leader should try
hard when he leads.*

Romans 12:8

BE A LEADER

Some people are leaders. They like to take charge. Some people are followers. They want someone else to be in charge.

Are you a leader or a follower? Before you answer, let's talk about leaders. Being a leader may not be what you think. A good leader doesn't just boss people around. A good leader doesn't have to yell. A good leader doesn't sit back while others do the work.

A good leader is a servant. Does that surprise you? It surprised us. But it's true. A good leader is someone who serves others. Bad leaders want others to serve them.

The greatest leader ever was Jesus Christ. Jesus never ran a company. Jesus wasn't a boss. Jesus wasn't a president. But Jesus knew how to lead people.

Jesus did this by serving them. He washed the feet of His disciples. He healed the sick. He fed the hungry. He felt sorry for the poor. Jesus told His followers: "The greatest among you should be like the youngest, and the leader should be like the servant" (Luke 22:26).

Now you can answer the question. "Do you want to be a leader or a follower?" Here's a good rule: You can be a leader if you follow Jesus. And you will follow Jesus if you serve others.

...IN THE SMALL STUFF

- Good leaders help others do their best.

- You will help others do their best by serving them.

- Good leaders follow other leaders.

- A good way to lead is to be a good example.

LET'S TALK ABOUT THE

SMALL STUFF

- Besides Jesus, who is the greatest leader in the world today?

- When is the last time you really served somebody? What did you do?

- List the names of three people you can serve this week.

*"You cannot serve
both God and money."*

Luke 16:13 NLT

GOD AND MONEY

Everybody needs money. But money can hurt people. Jesus talked a lot about money. He knew how money can hurt people.

Money isn't bad. What is bad is when people love money more than anything else. The love of money makes people selfish. Being selfish hurts other people. The love of money makes people cheat. Cheating hurts other people. The love of money makes people lie. Lying hurts other people.

The love of money can also keep us away from God. People get so busy trying to make more money that they don't have time for God. This is bad. Jesus said, "It is worth nothing for a man to have the whole world, if he himself is destroyed or lost" (Luke 9:25).

People think that more money will make them feel better. This is not true. Money does not buy happiness.

We need to remember that God gives us everything we have—including our money. He owns all of it—and we should give some of our money back to Him.

We need to be wise about money. But we also need to trust God for everything. When we put God first—in the small stuff as well as the big stuff—He promises to take care of us.

...iN THE SMALL STUFF

- Treat your money as if it belongs
  to God. It does.

- From every dollar you earn, save some
  and give some to God.

- You won't worry about money if you
  trust God.

- Watch the pennies
  and the dollars will
  take care of themselves.

LET'S TALK ABOUT THE
SMALL STUFF

- What is the most money you ever earned? What did you do to earn it?

- What is the biggest amount of money you ever received as a gift?

- Do you think God needs our money? Why or why not?

*Those who help others
will themselves be helped.*

Proverbs 11:25

BE GENEROUS

Do you know what it means to be generous? It means you give away something that's important to you.

Some people give away stuff they don't want any more. That can be helpful. But it isn't generous. Generosity isn't giving away your old clothes. Generosity isn't giving away the bike you don't want anymore. Generosity is giving away something you really like. Sometimes that is hard. But it's the right thing to do.

Giving your money away can be a generous thing. But sometimes generosity is much

more. Using your time to help people is generous. Pulling weeds for an elderly person is generous. Teaching someone to read is generous.

You need to give away your time and talents as well as your money. The Bible tells you to "do good and to be rich in doing good deeds" (1 Timothy 6:18).

Generosity also involves your attitude. Don't give something away just to impress others. This is the wrong attitude. Give things away to help others. Don't take credit for your generosity. God wants you to give Him the credit. Don't give your time or money away if it makes you grumpy. God loves a happy giver.

...IN THE SMALL STUFF

- Money is no good if you can't give it away.

- God is more interested in your heart than your wallet.

- Give the gift of time. It's more valuable than money.

- When you give something away, expect nothing in return.

LET'S TALK ABOUT THE
SMALL STUFF

- When is the last time you were generous to someone? How did you feel?

- When is the last time someone was generous to you? How did you feel?

- Why is time more valuable than money?

If anyone thinks
he is important
when he is really not,
he is only fooling himself.

Galatians 6:3

KINDNESS IS COOL

It's one thing to be generous to someone. It's another thing to be kind. You can be generous to someone you have never met. He could be a missionary in Africa. She could be a hungry child in India. You can be generous to people you do not know. God likes it when you are generous.

You can show kindness to someone you know. She could be your best friend. He could be a new kid in school. Or she could be someone you don't even like. God likes it when you are kind.

Kindness means you see the best in other people. Kindness means you look past the outside and look on the inside.

That's what God does. He sees all people the same way on the outside. The inside is what matters to God. He cares about the heart. That's where God looks—and that's where God wants us to look.

You are kind to others when you look at them and love them like God does. If they need help, you help them. If they are hurting inside, you say kind words. If other kids are mean to the new kid, you are nice. God likes it when you are kind. Kindness is cool.

...iN THE SMaLL STUFF

- You aren't kind when you just *think* about doing something nice. Kindness means that you *do* something nice.

- Sometimes doing a lot of little things for someone is better than doing one big thing.

- Being kind takes practice.

- When you are kind to others, you will feel good about yourself.

- What is the difference between being generous and being kind?

- Think about a time when you were kind to someone. How did you feel?

- Why aren't more people kind to others?

*Then we were
filled with laughter,
and we sang happy songs.*

Psalm 126:2

LAUGH AND PEOPLE LAUGH WITH YOU

Laughter is like medicine. That doesn't mean you can take a laughing pill or drink laughing syrup. Laughter is natural. It has no side effects (except when your side hurts).

Laughter makes you feel better. Laughter keeps you from getting nervous. Laughter does a body good.

Tell your parents to laugh more. Tell your dad that laughter is good for his blood pressure. Tell your mom that laughter helps her to think better. Tell your brother or sister that laughter is better than locking you in the basement. This may not work, but it's worth a try.

What makes you laugh? Do other people make you laugh? Try not to laugh at people. Making fun of people and then laughing isn't a good kind of laughter. It is better to laugh with people.

If you want to laugh at someone, laugh at yourself. People like it when you can laugh at yourself. It makes them feel better. They want to be your friend. Laughing at yourself doesn't mean you have to always be funny. It just means that you don't take yourself too seriously.

Laughter is the secret to a happy life. People don't stop laughing because they grow old. They grow old because they stop laughing. The more you laugh, the longer you will last.

...IN THE SMALL STUFF

- You will always have something to laugh at if you can learn to laugh at yourself.

- There are two things you should not hold back: sneezes and laughter.

- Laugh at yourself as much as others do.

- If you don't think God has a sense of humor, look in the mirror.

LET'S TALK ABOUT THE
SMALL STUFF

- What is the funniest joke you ever heard?

- Can you think of a time when it's not good to laugh?

- Why do some people take themselves too seriously?

*"Don't judge
other people,
or you will
be judged."*

Matthew 7:1

TAKE THE LOG OUT OF YOUR EYE

Nobody likes a critic. Okay, so maybe we don't mind movie critics. They help us weed out bad movies from good movies. That's not the kind of critic we're talking about.

The kind of critic nobody likes is someone who criticizes other people. This kind of critic will say, "I don't like your shoes," or "You talk funny." This kind of criticism is personal. And it can hurt.

Usually we criticize the small stuff in other people. Jesus said it's like noticing a speck of sawdust in someone else's eye. Jesus said we should remove the log sticking out of our own eye before criticizing the sawdust in someone else's eye.

We all have logs in our eyes. These logs are things we do that hurt other people. We need to remove the logs so we can be better people. Judging other people is a log (judging is another word for criticizing). You can remove the judging log by encouraging others instead of criticizing them. Saying mean things about people behind their backs is another log. You can remove this log by being kind to others.

Pray and ask God to help you remove the logs from your eyes. The logs don't just hurt others. They hurt you, too.

...IN THE SMALL STUFF

- Praise people more and criticize them less.

- You can't take back angry words.

- Two of the best words you can say are: "I'm sorry."

- People criticize others in order to feel better. Why is this a bad thing?

- Have you ever noticed a "speck of sawdust" in someone else? Do you have any "logs" in your own eyes?

- How can God help you to take the logs from your eyes?

*Your love
must be real. . . .
Love each other like
brothers and sisters.*

Romans 12:9–10

iT TAKES TiME
TO MAKE FRiENDS

People are busier than ever before. In the old days (when your parents were kids), people didn't have computers or cell phones. They didn't have to check their E-mail and phone messages. They had more time.

Today everybody is so busy. They are so busy that they have to drive and talk on the phone at the same time. Now some cars have computers. Now people can drive and talk on the phone and use a computer all at once. That is busy!

There are some things you can't do when you are busy. Making friends is one of those things. You can meet a friend in a hurry. But you can't make a friend in a hurry. It takes time to make friends.

Making friends is like growing a fruit tree. First you have to plant the tree. When you plant a friendship, you find things you have in common with your friend. It takes time for the tree to grow. You can't force it. The same is true with friendships.

Finally the tree grows fruit. A friendship grows fruit, too. Two people can enjoy the fruit of friendship.

God likes it when we take time to make friends. And He likes it when we take time to make friends with Him.

...iN THE SMaLL STUFF

- Spend more time with people
  than with things.

- A friend is someone who lifts others
  up instead of tearing them down.

- Friends stick up for each other.

- A tree doesn't grow overnight—
  and neither does
  a friendship.

LET'S TALK ABOUT THE
SMALL STUFF

- Who is your best friend? Why are you such good friends?

- What happens when you are too busy to make friends?

- Draw a picture of a healthy fruit tree. How can a friendship be like that tree?

Try to learn
what pleases the Lord.

Ephesians 5:10

WHO DO YOU WANT TO BE?

Sometimes grown-ups will ask you: What do you want to be when you grow up? We want to ask you a different question: Who do you want to be when you grow up?

What you want to be refers to the things you do. After you finish school and go to college, you can be a teacher, a scientist, a lawyer, a secret agent, a social worker, or just about anything you want.

Who you want to be refers to the person you are. You can be a person who is honest. You can be a person others can trust. You can be helpful to others. You can be loving. And you don't have to wait to finish college to be that way. You can start right now.

It's fun to think about what you want to do. But that can wait. You should not wait to think about who you want to be. That is because who you are is more important than what you do. What do you think about who you want to be?

God has some ideas. He has shared them in His Word, the Bible. Look up Galatians 5:22–23 in your Bible. Here you will find these things: love, joy, peace, patience, kindness, goodness, faithfulness, gentleness, and self-control.

The Bible calls these the "Fruit of the Spirit." God wants you to grow this kind of "fruit" in your life. This is who God wants you to be.

...IN THE SMALL STUFF

- The person you will be in the future will be a lot like the person you are now.

- The things you do come out of the person you are.

- God cares more about who you are than what you do.

LET'S TALK ABOUT THE
SMALL STUFF

- What do you want to be when you grow up? (It's okay if you don't know yet.)

- Why does God care more about who you are than what you do?

- Do you think God also cares about what you do? Why or why not?

*We are the
sweet smell of Christ
among those who are
being saved and among
those who are being lost.*

---

2 Corinthians 2:15

DO YOUR BEST TO SMELL GOOD

Have you ever smelled something really bad? Rotten eggs smell bad (make a face and say "Eeeeeyouuuuu"). Bad breath smells bad (that's why they call it bad breath). A nervous skunk smells bad. Teenage boys can smell bad (especially if they are nervous or forget to put on deodorant).

How about you? How do you smell? You probably smell pretty good. You don't need deodorant—yet. You don't have to worry about smelling bad (unless you stepped in something gross on the sidewalk).

There's another kind of smell people have. It has nothing to do with bad breath or stinky feet. This smell is spiritual. This is the kind of smell you should think about.

You can have a sweet spiritual smell if you know God as a friend. But you must let Jesus live through you. If you ask Him, Jesus will help you to be like Him. He will help you to be kind, loving, helpful, and forgiving. Those things smell really good to other people whether they know God or not.

If you don't let Jesus live through you, you might be mean, jealous, hurtful, and critical. Those things don't smell so good, especially to people who don't know God.

Jesus can't help you with smells on the outside. But He can help you smell good on the inside. And that's the best smell of all.

...IN THE SMALL STUFF

- People will listen to you more
  if you smell good on the inside.

- Jesus will help you smell good
  spiritually if you ask Him.

- God will use us to help others
  if we have a sweet spiritual smell.

LET'S TALK ABOUT THE
SMALL STUFF

- Sometimes the things you say can smell good. Can you think of some good-smelling words?

- Scientists say that your nose has a memory. What do you think this means?

- What if we told you: "God Is in the Smell Stuff." What does that mean?

Keep your lives
free from the love of money,
and be satisfied with what you have.

Hebrews 13:5

SMART ABOUT MONEY

Aren't you glad that you don't have to be concerned about money? Other people—like your parents—are concerned about money. They want to take care of you and your family. You should thank your parents for taking care of the family money.

You probably have some money of your own. You might get money on your birthdays. You might get money at Christmas. You might get money for doing chores around the house. You might even get money for losing a tooth.

What do you do with your money? Are you smart about it? Do you spend all the money people give you? Do you spend all the money you earn?

Spending money is fine, as long as you don't spend it all. It isn't very smart to spend all your money. It is smart to save some of the money you get.

Here's a good plan for your money. Each time you get ten dollars, save a dollar and give a dollar to God. You can save your money by setting up a savings account at the bank. Your parents can help you do this. You can give money to God by putting it in the offering at church.

God doesn't need your money. But He likes it when you give some of it back to Him. That's what people who are smart about money do.

...iN THE SMALL STUFF

- Money won't make you happy,
  but it can make you unhappy.

- The person who always wants more
  money will never have enough.

- Everything we have comes from God.

- Giving money to God helps others.

LET'S TALK ABOUT THE
SMALL STUFF

- What's the most money you ever got at one time?

- Do you have a savings account? Why is it a good idea to save money?

- What does it mean to be stingy? Is that a good idea? Why or why not?

*Faith means being sure
of the things we hope for
and knowing that something
is real even if we do not see it.*

Hebrews 11:1

HAVE FAITH IN GOD

There are many mysteries in life. For example: Why doesn't glue stick to the inside of the bottle? Or how about this one: Why isn't there any ham in a hamburger?

These are fun mysteries. There are also some serious mysteries, such as the mysteries about God. God is bigger than anything. God is stronger than anything. God is smarter than anything. Yet we can't see God. How can this be?

God knows how many hairs are on your head. How does He know that? God can hear every prayer of every person praying to Him at the same time. How can He do that? God knows everything you do before you do it. But He allows you to make your own choices. How is this possible?

We don't know. People even smarter than us don't know (believe us, there are plenty of people smart than us). These things are mysteries.

You may not know everything about God. But you know enough to trust Him. You can trust God to take care of you right now. You can trust Him to guide you in the future.

When you trust God, you have faith. Faith doesn't mean you can prove stuff about God. Faith means you believe that what God says in the Bible is true.

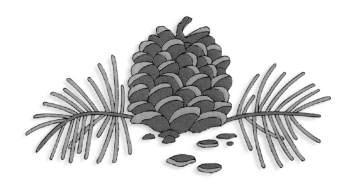

...IN THE SMALL STUFF

- Before you were born, God knew who you were.

- Trust God in everything, especially the small stuff.

- God is one mystery you can live with.

- This is not a mystery: God loves you.

LET'S TALK ABOUT THE
SMALL STUFF

- Name something besides God that you have faith in.

- How do you know God exists?

- Is there something in the future that you are not sure about? What is it? Can God handle it?

*God places
the lonely in families.*

Psalm 68:6 NLT

FAMiLiES ARE FOREVER

God loves families. He created families so we wouldn't be lonely. Just think how lonely you would be if you did not have your family. God created families so we could be with Him forever in heaven. Satan knows this. That's why Satan hates families.

Satan is the devil. He wants to destroy families. All through the Bible you can see how Satan has been trying to do this:

- Satan tempted Adam and Eve, the first parents, to disobey God and ruin their lives. But God forgave them.

- When Moses was born, the king tried to hurt God's people by killing all the baby boys. Satan wanted to destroy the family, but God saved Moses and His people.

- When Jesus was born, King Herod tried to destroy Him by having all the baby boys killed. But God saved Jesus so He could save us.

Satan has always wanted to destroy families. God has always wanted to save them. Without the family and without God, we could not be saved.

God loves you and He loves your family. He knows everything about your family. He knows the small stuff and the big stuff. Thank God for your family.

...IN THE SMALL STUFF

- Be as kind to your family as you are to your friends.

- Friendships come and go. Families are forever.

- The best way to know God is through your family.

LET'S TALK ABOUT THE
SMALL STUFF

- Say something good about each member of your family.

- What are some important things you can do for your family?

- What does it mean to be part of God's family?

A friend loves you
all the time.

Proverbs 17:17

BE A GOOD FRIEND

Earlier in this book we talked about making friends. Now we want to talk about being a friend.

It is easier to make a friend than to be a friend. That's because being a good friend takes time and hard work and sacrifice. It is hard to be a friend to a lot of people. It is better to have a few really good friends you care about than lots of friends you don't like that much.

You must be willing to show your friends how to do stuff. Are you good at video games? Then you should teach your friends how to be good. Are you good at math? Then you should teach your friends how to be good. This takes time.

You must be willing to learn from your friends. Learning from friends means you admit that they are better than you are at certain things. This takes hard work.

You must be willing to share your stuff with your friends. You need to help them when they need help. This takes love and sacrifice.

Putting your time and effort and love into a few good friendships is like putting money in the bank. The more you put in, the more you'll get back.

...IN THE SMALL STUFF

- Be loyal to your friends.

- Stick up for your friends when others tear them down.

- It's good to have some friends older and some friends younger than you.

- Pray for your friends. Ask your friends to pray for you.

LET'S TALK ABOUT THE
SMALL STUFF

- How can you be a better friend?

- What is something you can teach your friends?

- What is something you can learn from your friends?

Don't brag about tomorrow; you don't know what may happen then.

Proverbs 27:1

ENJOY GOD TODAY

Our time together in this book is almost over. We would love to be with you so we could talk about God together. We would love to hear how God is in the small stuff of your life every day. We would love to tell you how God is in the small stuff of our lives.

Our prayer for you is that you get to know God better each day. It's easy to do this. You just enjoy God every today.

You can't change yesterday. Only God knows about tomorrow. So today is the only day you have to enjoy God.

Here is how you enjoy God today:

- Remember how God helped you
  in the past.

- Believe that God will help you today.

- Have faith that God will help you
  in the future.

You can do this every day: remember, believe, have faith. This will give you hope. This will help you enjoy God today.

...IN THE SMALL STUFF

- Live life on purpose, not by accident.

- Always be positive.

- Instead of always asking "Why?" sometimes ask "Why not?"

- Don't always do the easiest thing. Always do the best thing.

- What is the best thing about this day?

- How can you be more positive about life?

- What is the best thing God ever did for you?

"I say this because
I know what I am planning
for you," says the Lord.
"I have good plans for you,
not plans to hurt you.
I will give you hope
and a good future."

Jeremiah 29:11

GOD IS IN
THE SMALL STUFF

It's easy to find God in nature. God is in the booms of a thunderstorm. God is in the rainbow after a storm. God is in the quiet of a moonlit night.

It's easy to find God in people. God is in the birth of a baby. God is in your dad's new job. God is there when your sister graduates from high school.

Seeing God in the big stuff in life is easy. It's harder to see God in the small stuff. But He is there in the smallest parts of your life.

God is there when you are worried about school. God is there when you are trying to make the soccer team. God is there when a friend hurts your feelings.

God is with you when you get up in the morning. He is still with you when you go to bed at night. God watches over you when you sleep. Nothing is too small for God.

God knew all about you even before He made the world. God has plans for you. He wants you to love Him and He wants you to love others. God wants you to enjoy Him every day. God wants you to know that He has thought up a wonderful future for you. Nothing is too small for God.

Live each day knowing that God is with you in the small stuff as well as the big stuff of your life.

...IN THE SMALL STUFF

- Thank God for the small stuff as well as the big stuff.

- Thank God every day for His gifts.

- As you go through the day, look for ways to please God.

- Be teachable every day.

- Talk about something big in your life that God helped you with.

- Talk about something small in your life that God helped you with.

- What are you most looking forward to as you grow older?

ALL ABOUT
BRUCE & STAN

Bruce Bickel used to be a comedian. But he wasn't very funny. So he decided to become a lawyer. People still laugh at him. But at least he gets paid. Bruce loves his wife (he has one), and he loves his kids (he has two).

Stan Jantz used to work in a bookstore. But he read too many books. So now he works with computer software. Stan also loves his one wife and his two kids.

Bruce and Stan love to write books. They have written more than thirty. *God Is in the Small Stuff* is their most popular book. They hope *God Is in the Small Stuff for Kids* is even more popular.

The guys would love to hear from you. You're welcome to send them an E-mail at: guide@bruceandstan.com. Or you can write them a letter at: Bruce & Stan, P.O. Box 25565, Fresno CA 93729.

You can also check out Bruce & Stan's Web site at: www.bruceandstan.com.

ALL ABOUT
PHIL SMOUSE

Phil Smouse wanted to be a scientist. But scientists have to do a lot of math. So Phil decided to draw and color instead. He and his wife have two kids who they love with all their heart.

Phil loves to tell kids just like you all about Jesus. He would love to hear from you today! You can send him an E-mail at: philsmouse@hotmail.com. Or get out your markers and crayons and send a letter (or picture!) to:

Phil A. Smouse, Barbour Publishing, Inc. 1810 Barbour Drive, Uhrichsville OH 44683, and the good folks at Barbour will be sure to pass it along.